SERENADE

Also by Bill Berkson:

Saturday Night: Poems 1960–61, 1961, 1975
Shining Leaves, 1969
Two Serious Poems & One Other, with Larry Fagin, 1971
Recent Visitors, with George Schneeman, 1974
Ants, with Greg Irons, 1974
100 Women, 1974
Enigma Variations, with Philip Guston, 1975
Blue Is the Hero (Poems 1960–1975), 1976
Red Devil, 1983
Start Over, 1983
Lush Life, 1984
Young Manhattan, with Anne Waldman, 1999
A Copy of the Catalogue, 1999

SERENADE

POETRY AND PROSE 1975–1989

Bill Berkson

DRAWINGS BY JOE BRAINARD

ZOLAND BOOKS

Cambridge, Massachusetts

First edition published in 2000 by
Zoland Books, Inc.
384 Huron Avenue
Cambridge, Massachusetts 02138

Cover and drawings by Joe Brainard, courtesy Special Collections,
Mandeville Library, University of California, San Diego.
By permission of the estate of Joe Brainard.

FIRST EDITION

Printed in the United States of America

07 06 05 04 03 02 01 00   8 7 6 5 4 3 2 1

This book is printed on acid-free paper, and its binding materials
have been chosen for strength and durability.

Library of Congress Cataloging-in-Publication Data

Berkson, Bill.
Serenade : poems and prose, 1975–1989 / Bill Berkson;
drawings by Joe Brainard.—1st ed.
p. cm.
ISBN 1-58195-016-0 (alk. paper)
I. Title.
PS3552.E7248 S47 2000
811'.54—dc21
99-089811

The poems and extended prose in this book were written in Bolinas, California, and Southampton, New York, in the years 1975–1989. Versions of some of them appear in the chapbook *Red Devil* (Smithereens Press, 1983), in *Lush Life* (Z Press, 1984) and in the following magazines and anthologies: *United Artists, Calafia, Poets and Painters, Volition, This, Sun & Moon, Big Sky, New American Writing, The Child in the Bell, Broadway, Acts, Chicago, Big Deal, The Turkey Buzzard Review, The Massachusetts Review, Shells, Best Minds: A Tribute to Allen Ginsberg, The Poetry Project Newsletter, Foot, L, No Difference Here, B-City, Bluefish, Blind Date, Gate, Ahnoi!, Cream Review, o-blek, Peninsula, Notus, Combo, Giants Play Well in the Drizzle, Penumbra, Big Bridge, Up Late: American Poetry Since 1970*, and *A Norton Anthology of Postmodern American Poetry*.

"Start Over" appeared as a Tombouctou Desert Island Chapbook.
"Red Devil" was published as an Alternative Press broadside.

Special thanks to Joe Brainard, Kenward Elmslie, Charley Ross, Ken and Ann Mikolowski, Michael Wolfe, Ron Padgett, the Fund for Poetry, Robert Butts, and Lynda Claassen of the Mandeville Library, University of California, San Diego.

Contents

For Moses and Siobhan

Basis

They index mosaics
Of who they have agreed to meet and operate
Out of webs of future nut-nurtured void
Denigration would be constant
I forgot whom I was speaking to for an instant
And would have been a bad boy
Had there not been brevity and merit in another
As the corner is a quarried conviction
Head bang over walls, chair

Cnidus, August 4th
for Larry Kearney

I put the candy in your hand and returned to my bee-watching.
Stamina could use tempo as a near-moral qualification.
Pleasant buzz, frightful sting. The *melteme,* bad wind, that
forced him to travel the lower coast of Turkey — Lycia,
Anatolia, Castellorizzo — instead of the better-mythologized
islands of Greece. Arcana accessible via salt marsh. And that's
where Saint Nicholas was born. "Me curator!" with a hip of
0.38 so's you don't take the pictures, tesselated, from the floor.
The door got repaired by adding to it. What he took to be the
sea as the overview of the Delphic oracle was an olive grove —
groves, really, sea-green, extending the slope to the real sea a
few miles out. "Wuz ya ever bit by a dead bee?" "Did you get
my rubber gloves?" The oracle put two dollars' worth of regular
in the Volkswagen and spun off, mildly.

My voices always tell me when it's time to move,
and where.

Domino

Mother and son are playing dominoes on the floor
in the cool of a bright late autumn afternoon, upstairs
of the little country house they live in. It is very
intent, like the eucalyptus. Two cats, male and female,
turn and jell on the patchwork Vermont bedspread. This
is northern California. Every ten minutes or so, one of
the players shouts out "Domino!"

Moon People

Two blue figures
synchronized to move
toward a blurred point
across the barest space imaginable —
will they make it?

Star Motel

Inside I could hear
a party of people,
the aimless cars
and in the middle distance
inexorable murmurs
of the ice machines.

From a Childhood #101

"You think the world
revolves around you."

I do.
Therefore, it does.

Had there been a piano in that room,
I would have studied it.

Mother's Mother

a photograph of

my mother's mother

aged about 22

delicate oval face

cocked to one side

her light-colored hair

tied back in a kind of bun

bright steady eyes

on the back she wrote:

"Your little wife Helen

Dec. 3, 1883

In summer or winter weather

Happiness means to be together"

then

"Married to Clay Lambert

Aug. 9, 1883

Photo taken Dec. 1883"

then

"Your mother

When she was young —"

Bubbles

I was a bathing beauty in *The American Venus.*
My dream of becoming a great dancer: How sweet he was then,
a brilliant, laughing young man of the world, his heart
so tender: "Get married!" I cried, bursting into fresh black
tears. Glittering white sequins: I put no value on my beauty.
Somedays I thought I would run away from Hollywood forever —
to Miami to Havana to Palm Beach to Washington, D.C., no less!
Now we are in the air, warriors of the sky, burning the beans
and *Wanted for Murder:* No rehearsal, no retakes:
His actors cry real tears: He wanted Dick to cry too and
Dick was not a spontaneous weeper: Breaking out of his grasp,
I grabbed a shotgun and killed him with dramatic swiftness.
That developed his character: Stars shimmering by beasts
in the black sky: His jaw muscles hunched closer to deliver
his monolog: "You're a lousy actress and your eyes are
too close together." I shoved him away, saying "Are you
trying to make love to me?" "Why not?" he said furiously,
jumping up and backing away to the door to make his exit.
"You go to bed with everyone else — why not me?"

Poem

cutting brush with a machete left
eye white cornea gets poked by twig
that was haste now abrasion seen
by doc who treats
eye-patch on and codeine in
codeine trips the psyche
home to daybed stretch
sentences that might be catchy slip
behind slow swirls magenta green
left eye watches patched
sea sky flakes magenta green
bird-size fruit flies slice
hotdog dinner right eye salted
watches sundown then "One Day at a Time"

Two Days

1.
Today is unsurpassed.
Rain in winter's jowl,
People in ponchos slogging through elephant fog.
"Your phone." "Don't I know it."
And somewhere out there a misplaced fire poker
gathers rust.
Here air, there water.
Formality unbidden spreads edgewise or else
completed a quarter-mile up where vines creep and pry
into bathroom boards. The grass grows.

2.
"Glass of retsina at Bill's. . ."
Fake dreams, reddened heat orb.
A word for the day abstains,
a trick mending. Pup gets bumpered, limps away.
Something we could do together, not sure what,
sitting and talking, aimless, adroit.
A day for obstinate, day for construe,
day the color and duration of a line by Jimmy
Schuyler in the anthology which says "I have nothing to say"
and stays bright and cold.

Voyage from Jericho
for Steve Emerson

Tying laces baby brown moccasins
Moses wants another strawberry
His lucky day, letter to Alaska
Set to mushing, Clover Lane
Our man in Anchorage, down chute in thaw
To bound and boo in heavy mountain cloud
Dishtowel bib face chortles prime for nap
Elsewhere's codeine, grazed harmonics, empty pipe
Swish, swiveling Alaska, land of land of sea
"Ready to dig a hole and get in it"

Familiar Music

A pair of dark blue panties
among hairbrushes.

Poem

Old lady peering into her P.O.
box — pink sweater, plaid skirt,
wire-rimmed granny glasses —
muttering "Harry. . . Harry. . . Harry . . ."

Baby's Awake Now

And now there is the lively sound
Of a panel truck heading due southwest
Along Elm Road, edge of dusk —
The densest light to see to drive by.

The underbrush has brown fringe
And small silent birds.

I saw the rainbow fire.
I saw the need to talk.
I saw a unicorn and a red pony.
And I didn't want any deviled eggs.
I drove home with my collar up.

We're alive. You do alarm me to the fact.
The light is on the window in the air,
And breath comes faster than the hounds
To sanction what remembered, what stuck.

Duchamp Dream

Marcel Duchamp and I are collaborating on a giant wall painting. Duchamp's part in this work consists of a talking portrait of himself — a profile which appears at the center of a brightly colored rectangle on the white wall. Using a long stick to push the colors around, I demonstrate the niceties of the composition to a large audience standing in semicircle around me. "You see," I say, "we (Duchamp and I) are much the same — but mostly at the edges!" Now the righthand edge of the rectangle explodes in a flashing white light which then "bleeds" into a field of dazzling pellucid orange. The room during this phase of the work has been almost totally in the dark — the only light source being the painting itself — its colors illumined from the inside. Now the room lights up and I am painting the four walls, running back and forth like crazy with my stick. In one corner I draw a huge black gorilla figure and pivoting to face the next long wall, I trace a black line punctuated with a thick gob of paint which sticks out like a fist. I pause, sensing this work is "a great success."

Dream with Fred Astaire

I'm in a large movie theater. I go to the john.
Standing at one of the urinals next to me is Fred Astaire.
He zips up his pants and says "I'm a loser!" I look deep
into his sunglasses, their mirrored lenses, and I say
"Oh you're doing alright!" He is visibly moved by the
open-hearted and believable way I say this.

Selected Dreams

At the airport with dark glasses.

Writing a master's thesis on the city of Nice.

A duel with electric irons as weapons.

Meeting Stuart Perkoff.

The Celeste Holm Sisters.

Anti-Poem

dust from windbag clots

days the human brain

scatters mostly

in a dry haze

over hill and sky

and love's colors

hardly distinguishable

from hay fever

sift

thus in a dream

I carry a white bucket

of shit and water

spilling some solid matter

into my vest pocket

and the villain played by Victor Jory

primps

and makes obscene remarks

whereupon I bop his

long bony nose

to a bloody pulp —

a fine moment of anti-philosophy

perhaps

but in the morning you are strange

To Lynn

The wind is blowing hard, and you walk
through its force to loose this morning's lost bunny
in a field of scrub. It's like everything is adangle
from this earthy grip. You watch patiently. The rabbit runs off.
I watch you. You are bigger than the bushes, and like them, not
to be bowled over, unlike me, by a whim. Head up,
you are fully aware of the clouds, and when there aren't any
you take in a lot of light. You give off a lot of heat in
the form of color. Today you are wearing white.

Lynn is putting enchiladas in the oven
in the next room, which this room,
or studio so-called, is out of —
I'll have to go out of one, outside, a step
or two, and in another door — all that
just for dinner? At times like this
life appears not hard so much
as complicated. Which is just a lie.
White language does that, to my
way of thinking.
                    ow the " " " " " "
o this typewriter just flew off,
the little plate/ ib/ key that was attached to
the rod part of the whole key
            and ow it's lost somewhere
I the i   er worki gs of this fucki g thi g
like "You'd lose your head if it were 't screwed o !"
This really happe ed.

old buttermilk sky

going to the big city

bye bye

Fourth Street, San Rafael

There was an old man at the bank today
Standing beside the paying/receiving window while his wife
Cashed a check or made a deposit she wore a light
Blue dress black shoes black hair
Not a sign of white or gray in it
But from the curve her shoulders made a weight sunk
Down to her ankles she was probably of a certain age
Though a few years younger than her husband
Whose ripened aging was no way disguised
A stiff olive drab fishing cap visor above his long bony face
And around his neck he had on one of those thong ties
    old gents wear
With a metal clasp at the collar and blunt tips at the ends
Loose hung sports jacket and baggy no-color slacks
    with a belt
He stood talking seriously to her about their money matters
And whenever he wanted to make some special point
He would place his hand firmly on her back and pat
    or caress it
With such decorum he would be her constant lover any time
Healthy wealthy and wise, and so it seemed,
Stepping up to the adjoining window next in line

To Marie Cosindas

The perfect pose
inundated by reflection
the group portrait groping for exposure
in the apartment circa 1966.
The world turns dolls into urchins
anemones, kelp, private mollusk & arachnid
till the string pops, inflection dings
subsumed
like dandies in shade
their handkerchiefs showing

Tint Guard

Big purple mid-October cauliflower incumbent grin
Steamed to pale green residency.
The skills have it. Gangs add a dresser,
Cabin fever and the like, and all completions pause
Penniless, adjunct on Quality Row.

So next year money will be there — gadgets
In the house turned topheavy between
False panics, no accounting for the burn
Or whine inside enemy vaults.

Assiduous *purgata*, legendary gouge
Blazed to keep from lugging
For such expensive tastes. . . .

Sweet loving must command new such limits
To a capacitance overwrought
As the powers that be, once slackened, represent
Each finalized trophy in the bin under tarps.

Ephemeral natter, what's entity to tell you when the kids
Come running wailing into your outstretched arms?
And where here are the hills?

Don't Knock It

for Lynn

Over piled leaves by the cement porch
trimmed and shook from a blue rug: hair.
The tangle upwind from where it fell,
where closer a branch makes a hard decision, shock-
definitive.
             Painting's trellis tide,
stemless seamless splurge and spray of
openhanded blue, pink top —
heart's constant labyrinthine shuttle.
Can't resist the way it floods, revvying up
for air: "The flowers are coming!"
A New Yorker's sense of distance: elbow-edged,
you take up a brussels sprout and peel it.
The right white gates span receptive
to your jubilant rush.

Slow Curve, Hampton Road

Snow elicits homage
from the honor guard
the outer gourd
the ilks ordained

time to get ready
to go up and get
ready to get
into bed

O rare-at-night felicity
featuring tan cardigan and tube socks

reversible me

Empire Edge

1. *Window Seat*
"We all volunteered for the job.
I want to be out there taking their calls.
As if what we think could matter.

It's only when they know you
that they lay it on you.
I made a total pig of myself."

2. *Getty Gas*
"Merrill, have you got a ten?"

"No, I don't have a ten, not on me. I
can go get one, though. I don't
have a pair of forty-fours either.
Just these arms: wave 'em around, all
by themselves, cut a man's
head off! Ha, ha, ha!"

"Entraining to Southampton"

Restorative
I'm trying on this suit of lights
in a seat facing the heavily lidded
man in a seat thinks of the painter Katz
an American Red Cross
green aquarium lights
tinted perspective prospect sufficiency bright

an ability to
change at Babylon

if my breath is scented as of drink
it's because I just took an aspirin

He's gone to sleep
behind the brown sweater
brown hand
pondering the nasal kinks
a staring too-imaginative BOND SAVINGS
(stars) — direct deposit — (stars)
What he saw in the moment he did in a flash
whathesawinthemomenthedidinaflash

after about five hours actually
allowing for chitchat

cigarette clings to the nether lip
facts are veils
"locked in here" (points to heart pocket)

roaring monsters parade between
and never forget it!

Delivery rush alert style sweetheart money

Give us this day: Marjorie, Randa, Joan,
Susan, Sylvie, Valda—the dainty import gone
missed backgrounds, pasting up others

sky remains, light flares
you would prefer coffee boiled and creation itself
"have at you then!" (Pa & Ma Kettle in Alaska)
newsprint taste of cheese strudel in the awake state
stunning a basketball wind

the coy Brian Boru
the corybantic sissy Benito Mussolini

& none of them are ninnies
none of the following:
The Black Jacket
Party
Canoe
Upside Down Ada
Elaine
Round Hill
Edwin and Rudy
Smile
One Flight Up
The Dancers

I'm not so sure about *Place*
(Moses would call it *Pigs in Space*.)

Lorelei

"One of the worst sins Dante could think of was to sulk in the sunlight. Those who did he assigned the eternal punishment of wallowing in mud."

"When I met _____ I really had the impression of seeing a saint. My first impulse was to put my head on his shoulder to get protection, which I didn't do."

A corner becomes the top (loaded dice?), and the space inside is fantastic, however dim.

Amid hordes of after-dinner sitters in "pumps," D.H. Lawrence gets up and throws a wet fish on the table.

"Doting is not loving."

Nothing is more perfectly obscure than the trace of intention and no mess.

"Another veering fit."

"Science is absolutely normal."

I really like the whole idea of art.

Because a part caught my eye that I thought I hadn't read, I began reading and read all the way through. Finished, I didn't see what I had missed.

Bad thoughts enter the food chain.

Mobilize versus drift.

You're at the edge of the crowd, trying to see what's happening. You start moving through, towards the center, the event. And everyone turns, adjusts — you're the center. Everyone else is "distracted" by your presence.

Process always leads to something terribly straight. Then it bends and we have shape again.

Think of nothing, they told her, and she did it to perfection.

Silence of a basement in summer, drifting over an impenetrable morass, a lot of throwaway space. . . .

Old lady behind screen door struck by afternoon sun: "Am I in here?"

"I regularly check the landscape in hopes of seeing what I keep reassuring myself is not there."

He groped to express a refined definition of what a man should be to himself. His thought became luminous in that dark field. "I've spent a glorious day in New England," he said.

Only now in my early thirties do I realize the incomprehensible pain of living, the inevitability of death, and the endless need for total illumination, be that as it may.

Those birds aren't the same bird. As long as the body is "experienced," it steals from itself. "I am of space, on time, equal to the place a feeling occurs." The stick figure remains, all of a piece, falling freely through the trees, very like light.

I am afraid I can be of little use to you.

A paralyzed Carol Lynley is booked. Crocker can't believe it!

The heart has reasons, the ego qualms.

Someone told him to shut up but his mind went on.

In 1936, Maxfield Parrish told Associated Press he had painted his very last "girl on a rock."

If the moon were the size of a quarter, the earth would be a nine-foot ball.

"The notion of brain pictures is conceptually dangerous. It is apt to suggest that these supposed pictures are themselves seen with a kind of inner eye — involving another picture, and another eye. . . and so on."

If you want to get somewhere else, try closing your eyes and writing your name with your nose.

Music is never content with anything outside while continually taking in as it goes on ahead. Only music gets through. Everything else waits in nervous contemplation of the door.

True tragedy is never to have appeared.

Primal California Dictum: "I came here with some catching up to do."

"The sky isn't *in* the universe. What does the sky eat? Does the sky drink rain?"

Unfamiliar person, familiar self. People in the theater refer to having found "a second home." Corporate bliss.

Run a pod for president. Faceless growth accumulates dream cells of total vote. Transpersonification of a blimp!

She's wearing pants tonight at the dance.

Anyone can anything anytime.

"To find out, add connecting lines, dot to dot."

Unconditional surrender is the final solution.

Talk, chatter, prattle, rap, babble, discourse, orate, blurt, hold forth, carry on, natter, mumble, pray.

I snap on the light. The waves roll in in Esperanto. These must be the famous California Irony Mounds!

When everything is turning upside down, try holding on with your feet.

Leave off dedication, enter sobbing.

Time blocks: Tune blocks of time.

The radiogram sat intently beside the empty fireplace. The gerbil began to walk around the bottom of the big glass jar.

The rate of the draw is proportionate to the speed of the burn, so you need more wood.

"When the heart discharges its load of blood into the arterial tree, it starts a distending wave along the stream of blood already contained within the system, a wave which can be felt in any superficial branch — in the wrist at the base of the thumb, at the temple in front of the ear, or back of the ankle on the inner side of the foot — as a 'pulse.'"

"The bank that served Lord Byron in 1812 serves Joe DiMaggio in 1974."

The world is waiting for the sun to rise.

An Atlantic Door

Sunsets in grid patterns

Whitewater saws

NASA checks

Eggshell junkies

Nasal focus clash

Blue Miami trace

Ms. Tut

Glass car rides

Twin bronze dimes

Mandatory brainsweat

Dune burner

Plumbers in their finery

Vying for the white tubs of Saturn

On Ice

Doors of jostled vicinity
An eager angle extending the sky a grey chasm
Tip of island street morning wash
A waking minute pointed to end quote
Squeeze left in diamond-beaded industry
Wedgeful elaborations desist
Shut behind us without saying
White lights from the powder-keg days

Drill

Fixed breakfast
Patch on old shoe

Wild oats stiffen
Foxtails stick

Skylight
Walleye

Webs
Whisked

Scramble
Disperse

Wistful
She's querulous

Hills
A fanbelt clouds

I allow as how
I recommend

"A pox on you"
The videotape crew

Try Again

Strangely remote or singular, not
particularly geared as me, that does not mean
you cannot touch me, you could watch me now
as my will comes running up the back stairs
with its platter of combinations. Come and eat.

After You

It is a very long walk
over hill and dale
and through the entertainment capitals of the world
to the dump.

Ocean and Grove

Popping gravel red bike goes, I walk
Sleek or chunky as trees, lupine throngs repeated
Boater iceplant, foxglove dusk
Mesa grasses ardent backing off an orange van

I got a shirt that fits, two feet to lope over
Looked into a photo and saw the face gaunt going
Not a destruction though, just one long face
Transient fair and pointless in a jittery wind

The cliffs lodged to waves melded hingeless
An edgeward dimming tinge
Glad hums in lunar abutment lace the rim
The smell of fennel is heaven sent

Burckhardt's Ninth

Paving the drink an elbow couple spans
Like the mantle of first meeting
Or how to make the jazz listen.
The record label on the lunge-stopped truck.
All God's bodies got coats, sheer Easy Street of bundled airs
And the filigrees arc lamps stand for,
The little bleached asides, nudged, padding, wry
Heights like neckwear in a bison's monkish glaze.
Permanent hair pegs in and bites.
Dark as police you trash to find a person dead.
A woman tugs at a kid, heels you could drink,
Twin nurses' rearview pair of backs.
Slab City's blaze flattens, flows
To shadeless: See the lady home.

Stamina

worn like sweaters against darker drifts.
He blinks in several places.
Then I wiped out the face
and when the face was gone
the skyline was standing
broke "in what
childhood scuffle I forget"

Annus Mirabilis

Funny, I'm capable:
If the house blew up I'd probably
do the right thing.

From Whence It Came

In a red chair with a toothpick
A space heater agitating
Between categories, scarcely heeded

Destiny slipping away

But you caught the culprit
Bidding him drink of the inland sparkling sea
All dressed up, real pretty

After 99 Comes 100

Coffee's bad for tai chi chuan
In Southampton we had a smoke alarm
California deems it plausible
To trade grammar for roof tar
The grand rondo for twilight and fog

Corny sentiment and perverted intimation
A stack of weathered magazines
Pet peeves of climate notwithstanding
Could shovel Adirondack or Mono Lake
But what did I bank on then?

This Election Day I tell you
I don't think there's much character in second sight
No matter how numbing post-verbal culture might turn out
Collectively sensible and chthonic
Whatever, but no

My loose foot stumbles overexposed
On the breeze-blasted mesa
A momentous urge in green entangles
Apes and angels, waves
For vocalese

But I want to live in this world
So long as it is just the one
Draped like mounds over an audible rest
That didn't get smashed in the process
When fate was looking

First Turns

In present comfort, a tethered box
how far and astigmatic seems the plea
beyond peculiars and asides
and quilted veneer wilts
staring into penny-loafer shade.
A titanic upset only chaos has delayed,
magnifying real cottage brands of stasis
moored in the vertiginous some floors up.
Familiar schmeer, by the lessons of which
an America dragging its heels foists helpless
love of circumstance as the match approaches
direct to "bat" — aroused utility blurring angle choirs
in sopping wet rain, prescient of how
to monumentalize the crypt.
Mad boy heart's face froze insouciant
white as long walls under the gun

Source

for Philip Guston

With thought first the dotted sun
Tantalized youth and darkens words
All the vain, some pure lump at rest
Sucking visible red ripe bone

Ways refuse to pull apart
Destinate melt-line tacks its comprehensive mound
My smokes rise high
Silent face that no less clarifies

Utterable reckon at perception's edge
Words consubstantial home to nothings waiting
Dumbfound here with air and hating
Strange to grow a bush of parts

I who am continues behaves
Like who isn't
Glistering shadow
The fuzzed skylight strikes

Oblique effortless to realize vacant
Building plausible dimension whence
Whole dawns premises exemplary embark

Stopping Is Nothing

Talk back to dreams even inside them
Spotlit rage tells charm's belief
Passion as a lattice levels air
What sun obtaining will enter your sheets
Burning like all get-out

The steady patter like an absence of remark
Matters much as the motive
For bad feelings in deep sleep
Or fiendish forgetting withal of it, them
Windfall of chancy flutter and flit
Whether or not the deep-trouble kind

Serious Moment
for Nathaniel Dorsky

Fair wifely thigh
sand, wave, puppydog

all presently within grasp
so like the song

thought Mozart
felt Keats

basic stately
neutral sadness

moment in the populous
hour-long movie line

trees rustled, swayed
stood lit-up

skirting sunk Utopia
on such a day

You Sure Do Some Nice Things

Someone crazy calls me I say "Ah-hah"
I have a jar of ketchup under my right arm
I have no inner life
No time to suffer shortcomings, someone else's
Morning after someone else's going away
Today they went away to stay
Furnishings deranged like looks in instant photographs
One frame we squabble, next we sweetly mend
Cooling heels entwined on a daybed,
Seemingly refreshed

Poem

How can equivocation happen?
Often mistaken as one

Notebook open, notes
interrupt one, "Go fish"

God's first elegy
"Then beauty is nothing but. . ."

Horoscope
says hectic

A bedtime message is
more direct

". . .tread lightly around
each other's systems"

Always forget *each other*
is spelled as two

Often mistook Eros
for a family story

Jump-start in any
tide stays put

Dark Middle

It's that time again
for the stars to be sent up
via dumbwaiter.

You Know What Crazy Is?

In the absence of delight,
the mind goes
and fucks itself.

Power goes off,
fizzles, returns, skimming
the surface, to place
a cigarette firmly
on its tip.
White tents are expressive
of an ulterior
but the frog knows when it's
still in the dark.

Filament ravished,
the flicker inspects bearings
to plot near leaves to the left,
taps the roof,
founds the trunk.
Phonics remain among the living
at some other end
but that's the brunt we brought,
the same any profile resembles.
The storm's document goes unchecked.
It has coffee.

Instinct

A mildly hostile point
breaks across the table
and is an organ of breathing
much as Hector and/or Ajax enthusing
over the Oxford Origins of Cures.

She always gets the dish the others can just about stand.
Then I'm sick to my stomach, writing off morsels the
    oven's already
turned down. Ever a tale of brooding capillaries
exposing a genre of matched sets: isocolor sweatshirt
    and grandma's
earrings, a fuzzy muffler and muff.

The table gets rounder than was guessed.
Its imagery's dowels are trained to bid us
become the masters of our age, not to act it.
No suspicious empathy, ambassadorial
to make solvable the hornet's trick of dream
as childhood's taller girls' in closets meant.
And if a tree falls to the ground
the earth will close and crown it.

End-of-Century Thrush

pins softeners
striation more pick-and-choose
face centrifuge outside rafters pillage
under dark to drink into my wall

old-wine allegiance
animals are balloon borders
refuse of cream rinse
the canvas further a canal did Braque

which but candle devil canard
his little light to sail outright
lugging peak of pale napes
"Get two!" nailed to a Yale thatch

Gurlie repairs the lull in soaps
"poor art for poor saps"
swish salute to particulars at sun flats
matted melted melded reeked beheld

early ignorance
chicken Kiev
"The truth for a day sat on his face"
mouth of June

up, drive
down, clear the navel
predigital in the bud
noyadea borscht-out!

Miami of Ohio-crowded curs
flinging sheiks along the Seaboard Line
extricable second rivers
erect success

fast first future for none
only to seem what becomes one
thwart bald spine
soothing the slab quarters

realism's liaison
disfigures the zones
snafu seventh-day trance
trench recedes receipts

"The Hoole Book"

Day after Labor Day first day of school
Balin slew his brother Balan
I because you

What is it about what we do
Militant music makes a muddy ghetto of ears

I'm crying all the time now
And faking every little thing

I say it a few times like this:
"I don't feel like going by myself to the bar"

Many roads do not lead to art
This gun is soap
To make yourself a rose, crush the package

You wish to cohere, so come here!

Sleep which defends no property
Oversimplifies the fabled
Unpeelable pit

I saw him lapping up dishwater from the sink
Now there's cat shit on my shoe and no floor

You seem to have laid claim to this puzzle
The ones with just words are plain bullshit
I walk in beauty for my sins

Being looked to being looked at being looked
Into looking away

Yet most of the ones I loved were there
Dismay sloshing the sides of the glass coach

Which were no worship but shame

Quel mess
I mess
One must
I keep the grammar in blood

A favorite plant has reproduced itself

No Claim to the Puzzle

Fragile as the glitter on Dame Felicity's eyelid spans
The visionary view. The day burns all costume and
Valence, face of the richly bearded sod.
Teeth showing and the eyes exact in it.
Great sky, greater pressure —
O perseverance the fuel and patience the fart
And pride the stripéd honeybee!
The farmer takes the hunter's wife;
Thus has prehistory entered your life.
You start anywhere. It goes a long way back.
Another heave at the worry wall,
Stucco postures on the heavenly bandstand
Where only tubas play.

Algebra

It cost the apartment tenant/owners in the cooperative $3000 per apartment to install automatic self-service elevators for access to every floor, plus the understanding that the former elevator men (operators) are not going to be laid-off. Now the elevator men will stand around in the lobby on the ground floor, sorting mail and answering calls on the house phone, and occasionally assisting the doormen — say, if the doorman goes to fetch a cab for one of the tenants or a guest. Also, closed-circuit television gets installed in every elevator and in the lobby at strategic points, levels of privacy thereby being insured or diminished, depending. It is work and ordinary ceremony. But at least one tenant believes it is unjust. Stunning to think of the men who taking parts as doormen or elevator operators and likewise the maintainance crew of handymen made the building their place of business for, in some cases, as many years from the time I came to live there as a child to now when I go there as a visitor. To the three or four who are still there working, greetings. One I would ask, "Do you still go fishing in Sheepshead Bay?" A couple of others still maintain their high Irish brogues. Charcoal gray uniforms with matte black shoes. And there was Eddie McCaffrey who would say, lifting his fist "One blow from McCaffrey would do you!" Figure with the A, B and C sides, 36 apartments. My mother lives in 11A. After 37 years, Harold's well-trimmed pencil-line mustache has somehow managed to remain permanent jet black.

Red Devil

The red devil perched with his sword
a little to the left above the profile of Dante
on the torn square of wrapping paper pinned to the wall
that shows a series of Italian cigarbox labels —
Dante is one of them, as *en Veil* at the tear-edge is another.
Dante wears his customary, slightly pinched, fierce "fuck you"
expression which is not directed at anyone personally, the viewer
but registers inner struggle toward thought and concentration.
The Red Devil was one of a string of Italian restaurants
around Broadway in the theater district circa 1950 where I
used to go for supper with my parents between Sunday movies.
It was my favorite for spaghetti and meatballs
and within easy walking distance of the best theaters —
The Rialto, Strand, Roxy, Paramount, Capitol, and Loew's State.
My father had lived and worked in Rome during the '30s,
he so enjoyed speaking Italian with the jovial hefty waiters,
and I would have Chianti mixed with water like a real Italian kid.
By the door and on the front of the menus was a red devil,
the piquant muted red of spaghetti sauce.
One time as we were leaving the place, getting on our coats,
there was a tall stately brunette standing near us,
adjusting her mink wrap. She was sexy, I was 12, I froze
and gawked. Then I noticed my father looking at her too
with a funny light in his eyes. I don't know which way my
mother was looking, but for a split second my father's look
and mine clicked, and he gave me a very knowing glance.
I felt something slip into place.
It was our first shared joke as men.

11:59

A door slams behind the thicket
and in the dark a car motor rumbles.
Another door just thuds.
Somebody must have shut it on their way out.
Like gangbusters the wall-heater fan comes on.
I turn it off and change rooms and put the cats out,
turn off the kitchen lights and go upstairs
to see if you're awake,
start talking.

Start Over

1.

I sleep late now I am fatigued. I'm over a barrel so roll me.
I hitched a ride, lifting a pool table with six other guys.
"Working / Do Not Enter." I said that.

Very lean today.

Cheese. Does he talk? No, I think he likes me, woof-woof.
Pea pills. Two? 1.W / 2.M. Would you care to ref' a game of
basketball today? This is juice. Vitt. What's that? Kittycat.
What's that? Cow. Show me the donkey. Donkey. Cow.
What's that? Cow. Where's the horse? Horsey. Horse. Whee.
We had upbringing actually, except North and South. "And in
the meat the snow." Beverage colors. Unplug jaws. Sure you're
not taking too big a chance? When do you think you'll start?
Thursday next.

Do you have an upstairs? Valentine's Day.
Glue Flowers. Would you like to make a flower? Be made a
flower. A baddy daddy. Why don't you color it too? Mine won't
work. Color it two. Go put. here's one for you. Pretty job.
Not off hand. Huh. Hi, Rosie. Wanna color? Do some gluein'?

I worry about them. They're trying to cope. I like Ivory too.
My condolences. Congrats for a job finely done. Shall we start
the picnic parade? Knock it off. I mean it. Getting yourself
all excited. You've changed. You're different. I'm not going to
spend the rest of my life on my hands and knees. It's not as
good as the book. Tiredest of "whatever's convenient."

Redesign, more a rebuild. Run-off. Additional catchment
chamber. Run-off at Louise Lasser. Could be goldfish. I shift to
change the murk. I have to take my hand away from my mouth.

I catch you at it. I write Big Band. Know myself like a book
and that's why I can't decide what to read next. Texts we've
met. I don't stand for the wrong words. The top of the chain
words. However I will you say don't, no money. From Stendhal
Love to *Northern Mists* a twist of the neck. Scratchless cheek.
Snow Lake. Thumb on trim-edge, other thumb gripping lip.
My own excited talk. There are no non-verbal experiences.
Results not interested at age two.

This business still isn't clear
to me. Can writing be taught? TV news is just specialized talk.
The gems are kept under lock and key. The key part of the
lock fits right in, pumping closure, little black hats.

The blahs.
When you come to know an absolute condition you are
probably past it. What's that you spilled on your shirt? Mnh,
Toothpaste. A town called Commack, a store called Bohack.
Don't make him sit back there in the guise of the topic.
The kettle rocks, strange to say. How come "is"es don't exist?
Except there's no other word to space it or an apostrophe seems
too slur? Asparagus, garlic sausage, hash browns. During
Pomp and Circumstance the Champ keeps a straight face. Only
a pygmy can kill an elephant.

Here is what I did with my body
one day. I go hunting words in series or My Prayer. Back to
base. Jollities enlivened the February superstructure. Kinds
of energy get swapped despite domestic superstrictures. What
is life together, something in the eye?

"You certainly make
civilization look silly," says Joel McCrea.

Moses sucks
grapefruit juice from a baby bottle I turn off the light yellow
pajamas over them a pink zip-up suit across my lap head in the
crook now rubbing his eyes taking the bottle from his mouth

extending it towards my right arm lift and lower him slowly
in onto bed "Nigh', nigh'" he sighs, I start for the door.
Trundle-bundle, the wardrobe of.

Katie knits in Heaven. It's
Arthur Okamura's birthday. I'll have to blast those walls all
by myself. Puffball slammed foul. Nerf. Stone cold egg. Bach
"Unaccompanied Cello Suite Number Six." Binder.
Marchsteria. Spell does. Comes the day eggs is writing by
hand in a book, a novel, and hidden however differently shaped,
it seemed that here for practical purposes, for feeling fact, the
shapes of the author's single self. But who is the author of
that thought? "You won't feel elated when you finish that
book." True enough, it is perfectly dreadful and hence exalting.
Inside the dome of total recall. Baby strangles cat. Bach
Unaccompanied Cello Suite Number Five. A pin-up with no
tack. Door opens out zooms kid. An entire new set of particles
is acquired. The dime kept spinning, the key at bar's length.
Mose shreds everythingshe wrote for three years running.
Thrum, sprightly bass. Time is school so it's detention for you.
Stay after.

The doctor has to drive some distance. Upper New
Yorican streets. (Dusk scene of other dreams.)

The boys are out
by the macrame. Boy, is he dumb. How'd you get to be so
smart, shoot with my hat? Fight between the cow and giraffe.
We need this like blue coat hanger. OK, a goat, bah! He's tied
up dead. You don't need two beds, cigagoo, cigagoo, slow.
We need a puzzle. I don't like you, truck, side go. I want to help
you cook, I'll start it for you, how do you like it, it's done.
Saywong, are you listening to Sesame Street? Hammer, I'll
help you. Put a dot on your tomato, put a dot on your grapes.
Krystal, luck, baby the truck.

Dry wash, slow burn. (Define

each thing by ingredients times use.) Sundown Jersey flats of
Lust for Ecstasy, Eakins's kids diving under Brooklyn Bridge.
Wild radish flowers Joe said let stay. Damon Runyon strictly
from Homer. Mose fingerpaints one shelf Crisco. Bunnyhunch!
Which hand is the nothing in? Still something there's the wall
to solve the man by lumps along the woodpile sun. Watch
your head.

2.
Dutch paint clay pipes. A stable margin of slow to no-go crams
now old clamshell full of butts. Big downpisser rain of pre-
winter natural. Today normally my sinuses would ache. They
just hit on another cigarette. No ache in sight and I am not
the victim to search for symptoms, regularly checking the
landscape in hopes of seeing what I keep reassuring myself is
not there. Search me, and the other of gigantic stare pursuing
an image presumably in the studio mirror unless naturally you
do such work by memory with eyes closed, inwhich event
bypassing the exact outer image marginally in favor of a funny
kind of — is it psychological? — replacement. A colorplate
anyway. Displaced.

A cut above the weather.

". . .bevy of simpering cuties in a bus."

Sunflower Sam.

First thing got out of bed and moved the chamber pot to
catch rain water pouring through the rafters. Then Mose woke
and we shared another early morning of insufficient restedness
verging on explosive discourtesies. Dagwood grunts. Mose

takes a pratfall on the spot of kitchen floor where a pan of
flaming olive oil spattered the night before. I keep thinking
"mop-up operation" as regards whole days. Backing up a
premise, reading the troubles women loving women make of
themselves in boring mock-Irish prose. Too much reminded of
the language's protective coloring. Mose pronounces a different
name-day for every day of the week. Today being Sunday he
pronounces Saturday and later amends that to Monday. I am
his Boswell as parenthood furthers constant biographical notice
and the distinctions come more various and pronounceable
than between personality-bearing and history-starved adults.

"To know a man now is above all to know the element of
irrationality in him, the part he is unable to control, which he
would like to erase from his own image of himself. In this
sense, I do not know General de Gaulle."

Sitting in a chair in
the middle of the kitchen, off the instrument. Smal dog jumps
off the edge of the book, cat to the left of my legs crossed. The
cat is now at the door wanting out. Out she gets and another
cat enters, brushing past her. Coffee water dribbles into the
glass pot with the hourglass figure. The yacht banged into the
boat and into the fish and into the soap isle! Wind is a felt
presence. Rain takes different diagonal courses down, hatchings
like the shadows along Rembrandt's cheek.

Silence that sticks
like where the key fits. The cheaper paper cones for coffee
refuse to drip properly, fluently, wasting it. Rumbling innards
and you go to the store. Small boy can blow a whole pack of
gum in an afternoon. The phone rings, stops ringing. That
sounds about right.

"Between April and August, Roosevelt,
Mussolini and Hitler had died. Churchill had gone, Germany

had surrendered, and the atom bomb had exploded at Hiroshima."

Get thee behind me, things that pile up! When there is no schedule and every day has to be invented to find use, then little energy remains to speak, much less to inscribe consciously, of the day itself. So I use sources, she says. Color TV burning the air before your eyes like a thermal mobile, the thin gray line of motion only inward. This one's in black and white: A man and a woman are trapped by a beefy maniac in a big white house. How escape? Pet boa constrictor's no help. "Imagine married life with a paleontologist!" Monster fangs, huge insect eyes —"Dynamite! Quick! The dynamite!" Man and woman climb up out of cavern onto sunny hillside, a fresh breeze blowing, and they look back: "Maybe it never happened!"

It is raining between the pages of a book. It rains on the book. The words, their "right orders," stay in line. The words are all water. The paper vanishes into thin air.

Nice summer weather, hot enough for swimming, long clear afternoons. Assume, taking the plunge, the first deep person. Dreamy Mallarmé seized beforehand, on ice. All there, nothing there, there there, all I can do to restaple it. Sing the songs I know: Here a chick, there diamonds the branch hatched and then the bristles of other trees on top of them and above those comes sky. Knee-high stove metal sheet cylinder, hole in it burned out. You have to break the bolts. When's nap-time? "Ee-Ay-Eee-Ay-O" he crooned, he croons, he keeps on crooning. We have come like birds to a stable strategy of crooning. Pauses arranged by soup.

Six A.M. the neighbor's dog gets to barking, then house dog in daughter's room joins in with a high yap, yanking me out of unspecified dream. Seconds later the baby starts muttering over bearcub-dotted bedclothes. Soupy no-sun up, chill Thanksgiving morn in the offing, recalls of nicotine spasms in getting to shuteye some hours previous. Police-kit motorcycle from maternal grandmother rolls over mattress the while, early-in-the-day kid of good cheer. Wife rises growling. Dagwood back into stupor an hour later follows. Before and after, later then now. Breakfast egg, grapefruit, and the end wedge of last night's spinach pie, and make coffee, all in a particular order not like a menu. Brisk bright windows blue sky. A big turkey from Santa Cruz thaws in the sink. Finished a letter and added several postscripts, sorted through self-important-looking stack of bills and select three to bring bank balance to insignificant $13.80. Other mail can thaw. Bandanna brushes ashes and unspecified grits from the desktop. Cigarette smoke a Tiepolo in the rafters. Yves Klein. Helene Aylon. Inside and out warm sufficient for an open door. The digital clock face flips over 2:12. A door thuds and somewhere overhead a motor putters. No, I'm not dead, I'm remembering to buy a new Bic lighter at the liquor store this afternoon. Til then, wrestle with the standstills, writing with a backhoe, and prospective, make notes on how to proceed with the actual panning.

  Naturally, the plain nuggets are right here scotch-taped to the bottom of an 8½-by-11 sheet, gravels sucked from riverbed and directed through sluice box ten-foot length bottom covered with carpet to collect fine gold. Blue your pan, says old prospector, it will hold the gold better. "I tell you this was a great thrill. Enclosed find sample of handpanned gold. Please say hello for me."

  I dream dawn on Fifth Avenue NYC. Street sign reads "40" but we're facing the Metropolitan Museum at 80th Street. I walk, turning uptown, on a series of white blocks. They are Rain Altars, on each is inscribed lines

from a new poem by T.S. Eliot. This poem is called *The Way*.
I see soul as a great storage like a present address book. The
Dictionary of As If. And Sutter goes berserkers. Heater off
now, he's blued, a small plane dangling, buzzing low as if to
inspect roof leaks, we got 'em. De Chirico dead, and R.I.P.,
too, Lennie Tristano. The day going on night, more irksome
or more sullen, no longer with us. Live dog among horseflesh.
Replays of years drawing to one close. Uncus, Chingachgook.
Composure, or so he thinks. "Here's his private number.
Be careful."

3.
Our dozes met. Lump matins in the glue works. Bound to a
ton. Eureka. "The world is too much fucking with us." Slice of
finger with my bread. Continuous taste of the usual Pete Smith
Specialty. Bye-bye, Toms. Embraced, they stray.

                                    Whatever
exists exists at all. Movies and mountains. The idea of a puppy.
It never entered my mind. And which for the child is easier
learning, patience or perseverance? My favorite lie: In prison
one would get a lot of reading done.

                             "All day nervous
wonderin' what to do. . . mighty repetitious." (Jack Kerouac)

"Enough money to live like people, y'dig."

                                       Find true right.
Can you describe clothing directly? Forms of dress. . .

                                       Mean
angel. Word sleeping on the yellow stain out of door. Nothing
to do in the house. Cat meows, kibble strewn to four corners
of a brain wave which locks, ouch, you can sense it. Roseate
patternings and the reflection has a flinch center. A coffee stain.

The fish died.

        Parsegenia I dream is a book by Turgenev. On the cover of the Everyman edition there's a cameo portrait of a girl, three-quarter face possibly a Vermeer. "Look for this book in London," I tell myself and wake up thinking "Parthenogenesis."

        Amidst light of bush *en la mesa*. Feel keyed to have made a mess of words. My little dog, Cuba. Little boy, Mose. Wife and family, matters of life and death. Orange pulp still clinging to the rind. What traits you acquire and which prove to be of some constant use. "Performance is simply the latest word for real-time activity." The car backed and the pipe hit. Write a friend a letter. A friend's house for dinner. How you like? I like fine. Thank heavens for dots.

        October 10th it's Monk's birthday so luxuriate, hah! October more, shirts, the mist, then heat-wave, then gets crabby. Dream Norman Bluhm paints a mural in the Bolinas post office. Norman has been divorced. "She told me the marriage ended eight years ago," he says. The mural boasts a naked woman fore-shortened lying on her back, head foremost in delineation. I read *The Duplications* drowsily by sunlight in the backyard.

Mean angel. Moritat. Sudden hungry dog. And eating a brownie on the stoop I smell oil. "There is no real content to our days, only our wild imaginations." Embraced, stray. . . Wait, first let me tell you what happened. Nobody's anything's everyone's mine. My loose tooth. My hammer. My piece of wood. The records. The keyboard. Everybody's ears. The car is our car. The mail in my box. Who else knows the combination? Don't hand me that that any's one though. I don't buy it. Let's call that perfunctory repugnance. Mose says, "Anybody Holly." Bloody body and wife and kids. Pushin' yr typewriter, hah?

Bright and cold. Please put my jacket on me so I can go outside and cry. The grease pencil melted on the cast iron stove side. Glass in there wears out so you expect it to last until it doesn't that's the lining, and the guy from Woodstock said the welding wasn't so hot.

Dream is, I'm showing Mick Jagger how to dance in a bowl of rocks. I wake up hearing "Beast of Burden" between my ears. Another showbiz Purgatorio rap. At day-care Moses bit Nigel on the arm and it looks like Susan is offended. Funny, you want real pain to be transformed into a conception two can share like pleasure "Yeah, let's" or "Yeah, let's not." But that's not in the bargain. Pain is really special. Think of dreams that entertain the fear of it but never see through to the hurt. Whereas you can have pleasure clean through and even speak of it after.

We both like solitude and we both like each other's company. Together we are getting everything but.

Fact is, I hate to talk turkey and cannot begin to explain the sorrows *in absentia* that accrue. I take them to be the opposite of my nature and lay no blame for their adhesive inarticulation. My address book is intact. The weight of the world is not sculpture so prefigured is it among the productions of a kid's crayon verve that we who pretend to know it tack it up inside the home, on the inner panels of front doors, reminder of what's in store if one should cross the line, e.g. go to the store, get chewing gum for the major genius.

A whole life is this click we make. Fumbling, pushing ages, hands and feet, brain and penis and address book intact. Ink stains your fingers as you turn the ribbon over looking to chance interpret the letters agglomerated there. I don't think Nicolas and Alexandra should die, no. Yesterday friend's wife had shown him a baby snake. Today he could kiss her ass. Can the job get done and never be televised? Leave the beckoning to us. A furry caterpillar traces lines dividing disks in quarters. Is this how you usually speak to adults? Give the gate a fair shake. I miss my fish. Energy translates a room as if the world were verbal. Seriously. Consider it safe from the whirl. Consider it dead. I recall it is not just you who makes me do this but also static. You flatter, you cajole, you ball it up. It's like there are (there are!) flies all across this page.

I am rubbing your shoulders by the kitchen sink when the water-meter man appears, gesturing with his clipboard for someone to go move the car.

4.

The weather in Ruysdael or Trenton. *The Great Trade Route.* Sun shines five miles inland in another direction. Guys on a cherry picker trim the overhanging cypress/eucalyptus branches and the wires hum. Indian Joe with his ears to the ground. Power grader rattles over new road. Pushing on forty. People lugging groceries home. They say money is hard to come by. He shows them how easily had it is, walking the length of the bar, sweeping all loose change into his hand as he goes, keeps going, pocketing it, out the swinging doors.

Regulating my mind like this in solitude — you'll never know if it's slipped — and the parallel world of people, "the people here. . ." Pleasant thought that some instinct's intact. "Human voices wake us and we drown." Imagine the looks I give out of *that* world as they go by in cars. And downtown Bolinas, guy tacking up Scowley's menu on the Market bulletin board, a few "Happy Hour" customers visible through the doorway of the Bar. A big blue Cadillac. The Shop dark, remodeling progresses. Big cypress on the hillside, Francisco Mesa. (Where, some years previous, a small blue pea-size beauty dot burst mid-skull flooding the sob-circuit.) Almost Winter Solstice, days seemingly lengthened in advance anyhow. Another guy tuning the piano in the Community Center. "Everywhere I go I know what's under me." Clara, light, the power or powder of wax, wax the color of angels, an angel's foot. Here air, there water. Eat this sock.

Now I know two kinds of yellow truck. A stack of *New York Times* tied with frizzy string to be trundled off, back of car, to Henry's Service beside the creek in Stinson Beach. Mrs. Henry renowned for her phone yells, pink house, sons who work the truck — Henry Henry, I once heard, is one — the serious demeanored cactus beside the perimeter foundation, lots of abandoned might-be-handy stuff in the yard. You leave the bundles of newsprint under an alder tree.

AARDVAARK RENTALS

Phil Bend
Accapella Gold
Adele's
Charlene Aetna
P. Aime
J.S. Ale
Wendy Archer
Leon Arrow
Jerry Barnacle
Schlomo Barnoon
L. Bent
Bill Bills
Robt. E. Boat
Bobo's Arco

Irwin T. Boop Jr.

Odds are. These days of being together. The best they have to give. Care and feeding of a bed of roses and the thorns. Bad bed has grains of sand to forestall sleep as caffeine has alertness, sort of, and fatigue, built-in. Significance admiring and respect endowed with qualities nearly in reach you latch onto, existing and unimpeachable as, say, a banana peel lobbed into coyote bush. Do they acknowledge heartaches into the chicken dinner are built? Dogs in throes over a dark bone. A part of two. "Back in the kitchen was what everyone had expressly sat down for." It throws them. Now you talk, dark bone. Rooms within rooms, the buzz of the personal, first star I see tonight.

The dog humps the cat, and the cat is female. I woke and thought of the New Year in pre-Copernican terms. Less character, less pre-bloated. Wired to the writing in the same voice or an adaptation. Whoever today writing in a woman's voice. A mousyness being. Against the gray sky the green trees in middle distance look black. The same but nearer against the black ones look green. Eight jacks and a superball. Thung, thong, thing. I stare through the lightbulb into thicket. Rain goes the windshield wipers, sh-sh. I go to the office, then to the factory, then to the Co-Op, then home to write. Heavens will not fall. A cruel proposal dating from the clearing 4 P.M. pavement. The duck's breath has played about the shadow of her smile. My, she's beautiful albeit out of reach on the other side of the mountain, to see plainly the advantage she would cozen. Men who drink slap their sides, the motor clicks forward, a sloshing like beer.

Going about her business in a day, and I'm a busy man. The space heater is turned way up as though it were cold. One hundred things meant mentally for

recall are (rip, foist) plastered over. They aren't. I don't see them
there, or from here. Idea lingered into recent times, for the rest
of my natural life whenever I get back to it. Red trees when
the light's below, looking for the edge and oops found. In the
diamond pattern I distinguish two shades of gray: one like
the empirical blur known to scholars as "California" or "The
Original Flake"; the other is like the North Sea of Henry
Heine's wild imagination, pure surface maintaining one eternal
stranglehold on depths deep down in which sense finds no verbal
junction, perfect for watching the sun die.

5.
On white paper film speaks, you say hello to yourself in skins.
Walking a light print dress on a bike seat wheels, zooms by the
tree trunks. Flashing the road past the grove. Address changes
outwards, so where'd that go? A shot like a flashback only you
keep staring ahead down the pike. "What holds these things
together?" "Celluloid." Big butterfly, you blinked. Say maybethe
creek ran after her. Fair, crisp, fresh, as in a rhythm section.
Let's talk business elsewhere. You are free to guess.

>   All this obbligato
>   He learned to read and listen
>   Lifting a chair to hit you
>   all in fun

                    October 18, I dream a big spider
tufted with pubic hair. Teasing harmonica in the neighbor's
yard scales, stops, says, "See ya!" "Don't forget to wear
your boots!" A late-blooming sun flattens near-sides of trees.
Quitely then a new voice shrugs "Forget it." How so?
Hello — Hello — Hello. How are you? I am fine. I — am

— fine. The floodgates close and behind them the waters
are brimming, a dog salivates. The dog is frozen in this gesture,
an icicle hanging from his chin and a block of cement chiseled
into the shape of a bone between big front canine teeth.
Whereupon she says, "I need a new Spring style." Start over
so you begin to see.

        For love and money and for George
Burns. TV pink aerial wags towards Orion, the California of
the skies. A resolute sense of scatter. She is at the front door in
eggshell ermine a glass of Cold Duck in each hand. Beads fall
between pinecones and mittens. Baby hollers in a field of Ritz.
The trio for evening and fog. The sense of them is Gothic. As
a couple they seem Gothic. There is something chill and stone-
hinged Gothic about the two of them. As people, coming on
really Gothic and bizarre. The Gothic way they both live.
Proviso, caveat, why the hell. Cold grapes. I believe that hand
from the cloud.

        The kids right the bean truck. Piece of mud,
a flat over wet ground. A Colorado flatiron too. High blues and
dry whites. Every day's a quake alert or summer mends its
oboe-shine. The topping branches gray off, a bug-strewn veil.
I'm not just grousing. Girl in a turquoise swimsuit on the beach
looks like my second cousin Mary El. Pointless feel of looking
on without words (or the contrary sense: "These are my
names!"), things in blinders slipping, going through one. Lift
eyes to trees, tops, walking, an obviously scary bliss. Light
colors of roses on a bush, paper trash in someone's front yard.
A beaut'. Ineffable's the base. Remember when a kid they said
I had a downcast look, staring on the road a few steps ahead,
supposedly introspective. Here it is since then and how long
have I been doing this? A little rod raised above the gong, a
straight blank whole.

        I've been sitting here. There's no you.

It's a possibility. The puddles glazed of thin brown ice. Mose up and goes to nursery school. Nobody's going to touch anything. This going bearing neutral off a working cliff. So I started concluding. They ask me and I write a book. I moved in and Jack or Bill said now you have a cabin. A roomful of haystacks I connive on the bias, hold large inventories and make do. Kettle, lantern, mouse, a ripple in the icetray, "I want to be a nurse." Bicameral denunciations that would sour a Doge. Another 'scape in car apple dawn. There is death in that sentence. Stars you see on a page blatantly do not remind of night from land. Likewise, when asked to introduce one to a group or one group to another, the names all around elude my saying. I want to say "You know *you*, don't you?"

Beer from Holland comes with rubber plugs. The cat moved too fast, the bird caught it. "Daddy, will you wash my butt off in the water?" May 8, Lynn and I get married at the Governor's palace. All set to cook the Nuptial Egg. But there's an extra fee for cooking it on the Governor's hedge, which burns in the process. We decline this optional pleasure, speaking with Mrs. Governor, the nice old lady.

If it rains in his brains the word for grass grows. Green grass water all around and under. Plot of grass, conspiracy to replace a lake. Beside the lake a sick cat will eat grass to grow stronger, more resilient. That is to say, the grass key. Extravagance in his rightful grass. The word for grass relaxes. Throws the magic switch. A man of keys, a man with keys.

6.
All birds fly to one tree. All birds go home. It's everywhere, that's something, you can't beat that. Thus does prehistory

enter your life. Old dark wood house, white wicker furniture,
separate room for stray cats. All you need is scratchpads.
Drawn to story alter middle of pose mouth. The sea is loud.
I want to say recalcitrant but the sound winds stuck. Instamatic
camera dangles from the draftsman's lamp. I like ease, how
come? White columns beside the inland sparkling sea. Short
and sweet, so a quickie. It goes a long way back, aimed at
abutting on the abstract express. In the Aquarium basement
we have chilidogs. Wettening cunt on some Australian
mountain long walk home in cold spray. Home is not a harbor.
Alice is hungry. The dog pees on a sandcastle. Surprise blue
indoors. The foghorn bends a blue note. Shower, dress, shave,
start cleaning up around the apartment. Acedia in the parking
lot of the Surplus Store. Vocalion of Mister Mustard in the
surge brown soup. I'll hire out as a flyswatter. Weigh out this
chair. A grown-up Archie Comic. You laugh.

> "He's loyal, devoted
>   in fact, he's a jewel
> But critical often
>   and that's a bit cruel"

A dog dream, large and fluffy. Dream I'm talking with Jimmy
about his new book *Other Sides*. Lynn tells me her dream of a
red firetruck on the ocean. In front of the truck stands a man
wearing silver- or gold-rimmed spectacles holding an empty
drawer. Dream I'm writing a story commissioned by *The New
Yorker* called "The True Romance of T.S. Eliot" which begins
"Samantha ran down the stairs." I dream I tie my tie. Dream
my mother is in a hospital in a state of nervous breakdown. She
is a young beautiful blond and we fuck. Dream the little white
tabs at the edge of the half-filled swimming pool give way each
time I try to hold onto one. I wake up thinking "Sink or swim."

A Paulding, Ohio, sign reads: GET RIGHT WITH GOD. Milky lightbulb reflects on milky coffee "001." Whosoever lists the nights   it rained. Each has a book and so something to drink. Last night it rained then snowed and this morning rain again, wet snow in patches on the curb of Hampton Road, slush for a saint's day like high school Easter vacations ever commencing with the last packed-in blizzard of the year. Blue-ice Elysium of Central Park, off-white rubber booties of Kim Novak in *The Eddie Duchin Story* At Eddy's Luncheonette the pickle jar advertises fundraising for The Little Flower Orphanage, burned down. Mose immediately interests himself in the predicament of homeless peers, stares for a moment at the small square sign glued halfway round the pickle jar, then pointing emphatically at the lunch counter, says, "You mean they're going to live *here*???"

Do women think in a calm voice? Does a bear? We've had to have a speech to the desk. An uplift, right push upward, pull back. No sleep to speak of rhythm, and now what I did. Proofread by sting ray, troubles on parade, 4:25 P.M. in Toyland, in disarray, in mileness, a utility field. White cabbage moth on the inside rim of the Big Bird glass with a bright pink wad of Bubble Yum on the bottom.

This is where I get off. Almost midnight. Dogs, dark, double ducky. Welcome to the Wonderful World of Family Living. I drove home with my collar up. In the company of only women, clam-shell caught in the blender, sharp and buoyant fellow. Lolls reading Paradiso. Scrunch. Peduncle. Scrunch. Tongue pressing roof of the mouth asserts connection. Don't knock it. Don't laugh, that's what you think. The received idea is parent to the old fart. The priest in the pit says, "Everyday life is Hell." "Yes, that's true," I tell him, "but there are transformations." Signs of spring. Piecemeal dither and a fire in the next house.

A dim metallic helicopter streaks past roofs along the shoreline, spotting survivors. The sky smears, the smear clears, now fluffs. To think something benignly simple, to wit: My mother made me breakfast this morning. I sped up and hit a dog. For shame. Attitudinizing don't pay. Nozzle in the shade, the earth and all its Pampers. Livewire kid puts arcane exuberance to the wheel of "Guts! Get it? Guts?!"

Assume the clerk. All this from somewhere I could use, notes mostly as I stir the potatoes or fashion a new zipper from the toes of the sloth. A peck from the supply wagon off Mulholland Drive. Waters of California run up the flag. The sea is loud in its mileness. Vizzi Red Creme Enamel says, "Going out to George's tonight to chew him out?" "Nah." "Mimsy?" "Yeah." "You're wanted on the phone." Six girls on the Long Island Railroad sing a song of their own composition, "Talk Dirty to the Animals." His poems are criticism mostly, coin of the realm. All that centrifugal influence of a stove. But I've been influenced enough all along. From first things first to the final finish. Whose dish night?

7.

I was talking figuratively about something real of course. Like, you are a kid and you *are* strong. Small matter that I can whip your ass or Darth Vader won't listen to the supply side of Empire melting. This is such a small room that I lose the extensions. What use is a phone cord if you unhook it? The way money works to pay spleen as I walk uphill with a recognizable later. There are those who gleefully describe a situation as intolerable and then devise strategies that are, at best, intolerable equally. White Shadow wants his brains back. Coalville, Utah, does without a one-way street. The phone booth at the corner gave the only light. Boy, did I need

to talk. In the knowledgable kingdom, things of its stars
receding, thin red reeds. Horsefeather sunset at Agate Beach.
In the garden, putt-putt, hear the light, the signed edition of
a concrete step. Things so stark in nature they recede. That
nudge tone, phone turned off. Surplus of cognates.

                                                           To you's a
useless trine. I need a whole new deck.

                                                                     Decision cantilevers
on the perpend to a one-way street. Road narrows to one lane
which is fast disappearing, classrooms in the deluge. Matri-
archal America. What if the house fell in a big dark hole right
now? I sat up in bed portending feminine/masculine in
mundane paradise. Four birds fly across barlines, followed by
five, four, unaccountable, a flock. But they're not the same,
I mean blameless. My love is not careless, even though it never
learns. A small red sore on my wrist seemsto be telling time.
Air matter water. A bedroom yellow with a Yale lock. Marriage
is that basis that mounting eponymous spot was hot. Was hot
you? I married a colorist. And honestly she looks to me so clear
I get ideas. Can you explain yourself to this life? Inroads of an
ocean that never stays put to become its name, slanting flying,
state of clutch. Rage chases panic around the bed: "Nothing!"
"Shut up!" "Real!"

8.
Enthroned in the bookstore, a clerk for the day, thoughts of
certain absent ones become group portraits of bodies, faces
known a few feet off the floor above eye level. The inner crystal
horde light presses, switch thrown, on air detected. Allakazam.
Quite a science, so reasoned and factual the angels are. "To
have something important materialize is not the point at all."
Now only medicines arrive in the tiny thrill-boxes decoder
rings once were dispatched in from General Mills. The time is

more marked, more repeated than heard. If you ask him he'll
tell you and then you'll never know. Electric tin can out of
somewhere, Speonk. In a faded code, the paint-removers try to
tell Santa's helper the way things work in a people's store.
You've got the right idea, Utopia, I grant you a phosphene, I
leave you Anna Schmidt's flats, three-chord Persian Gulf or
the "Now You Have Pushed Death's Finger Lobe" dream.

                                   To
touch only when appropriate. In a staring contest with the cat
I am always the first to blink. Would you let your child come
home unescorted to an empty house? The yellow machines are
shaving back French broom to clear the culverts. And there's a
backloader too, the purpose of which isn't clear. Chou-Chou
says marriage is unlikely for other than weird. Andrews gone
surfing. I seem to be tottering thematically in the afterlife but
that's mere books, music intelligently structured but not (bzz)
taken to heart. "We've got a lot of banged-up birds" says a
street voice. Luther Burbank invented the nectarine so how
much do we really know about Malathion? Do we save *The Life
of the Virgin Mary* for Larry in Brooklyn? He is the one that
calls her Honey. We all have to get up in the morning. "Honey,
I'm leaving now."

                    If I think long enough soft enough maybe
I could say, "Want to jack me off?" Nicotine and caffeine are
vasoconstrictors. Fear of empty compares favorably with fear
of none whatsoever. What is fear? An extra corkscrew for
the twist-off cap. It's only natural that I save myself to kill the
moment before it breaks the skin. Burning paper mirror, nice
new smell. Compares curiously with the high-keyed excitation
of credible rebuke running on empty five miles from head-
quarters or thirty seconds over Tokyo. Tenor madness. Snowy
moon inside the pinball whale. Alamo *amat*. "God help me,"
says George C. Scott's Patton in the burning ranks, "I love it

so." Same goes for New York. I dream Edwin Denby at Tie City, green sector (green, I'm against green!), Mr. B.-collar conceit, and the ever salubrious Smith Brothers. There is good, better, best, and bad, worse, worst. From bad to worse is acceptable. But the best is good. The parrot flies to the most sensitive spot. Raw nerve lands there. Good for you.

Ted wakes me up outside. He's singing, "Drop yr cocks & grab yr socks." If it's Monday this must be Korea and I'm an orderly shaving to his blaps. Fielding Dawson was the last one to sweep up around here. The whole bed's aroma of Ben Gay in deference to the lower back, sweet watery themes. I make a perfect U-turn in front of the post office and Don's Liquors and straighten out aligned with Seashore Realty. I once published my objection to a fence. Fern Road dozes in its kitty litter, a helmet with a faceguard under pampas grass, vacuum arrangements for coffee and tennis balls. Petty irritables take umbrage at greywater. Two more than one I turn into you. It's no hardship but what in dumb fuck's name am I doing with here what am factor of absolute importance to this scheme? Last day, no gold watch? Name brake, blame's sake at the battered gate p'diddle companion of sleeps. Phone rings Mose runs "I'll get it, I know it's for me!"

9.

It's just you, only me. Fuck Mexico. Coastal fog burns off. Kent Island gleams like Rameses ramified. Ebbtide's a marvel of slick dispatch. "I'm going to get my action figures." Shasta daisy pokes out of the berry vines white as a Tuffy, a sheer porcelain tremolo. Every so often she turns over, belly to ecru sheet, and reads another paragraph of *Lady Chatterley's Lover*. "No credit. Can you imagine! No credit?" When a clear solution of need discolors the eye of another, you cry. How you cry. How I wish.

Dan Rather, I hear, gets all the girls. Ashes, sand, clouds, incense, fog, haze, bubbles, froth, spittle, surf, spume, phizz, dust, lint, cobwebs, fuzz, gnurr, lava, calcium deposits, stalagmites and stalactites, steam, stains, sweat, mucous, urine, shit, boogers, earwax, dandruff, psoriasis, pus. Smoke, semen, and catarrh. Phlegm. Blood. Stitches. Ovaries. Brushes, bedsprings, old tires, sheetrock, compatability, mice.
                  Mr. Spock says, "Everytime you humans encounter a structure you don't understand you call it a *thing*."
                  Here's the format: Life won't come fix the car. Gray day, mind a-many, a mule train and overexposed. I circle myself into the 40–65 age-slot on County Library fact-sheet, quite a jolt. Pale ink effects gambol over textural densities. In Celesteville, a thing a day. Dagwood's suburb doesn't have a name. Peritonitis is not a disease of the gums.   I don't want to be left alone to live in peace. Flowers can't want to read.

> "At least it's clean"
> "If my thoughts were that gentle"
> "I hope you hated me"
> "Oh, only briefly"

Happiness, half-cocked moon, gentle innovator, can you write poems? Yes, much good it does me. These rocks have no madonna.
                  At the bookstore the point is we must stock more 19th-century novels. We can return last year's Dostoievski and get Balzac. It's hard to remember if there has been any profitable turnover in the area of, so to speak, Dickens. Bukowski

isn't moving. Used Melville sells pretty well. Nobody seems to be able to predict what people will read but it's plain to see what some of them are reading. Things by women get read a lot. Guides to Mexico and Yucatan are popular. Local authors are sentimental favorites. *Shibumi* is hot. Last year around Christmas we had a lot of dance books but only the ones with mostly pictures sold out. The big sellers in fact have been greeting cards, health-fad books and cucumber soap.

      The gravel has held. We're crazed infidels on the verge of mixed emotions. There is a strong possibility of drought. Lumps nodded like cat to slats under the Motorland sun. The meeting "and now we have this kind of set-up." It looks like we're on dry land here. A mirror undertowed in concomittant puree is unacceptable. The people must vote. The *National Enquirer* tells lies. We have had it up to here with broken promises. Tom likes Jim. He can see what he knows. Go to Gary, go to Gary, go to Gary, do. "If that phone rings again I'll kill it!" Music on the radio no one ever plays at home.

      July has parted with its kneescrape scabs. And outside everywhere the moon. I can't get off her. (How come I can't hear her who am her voice?) Dream I'm telling Arthur and Suzanna how it feels to be 77 years old. "No difference really, but look at this shirt!" A white heavy muslin, one hole in the breast pocket flap over my heart. While in the awake-state, I'm taking in the kitchen: Wide sight of whole cloth, chrome, tile, wood, stainless entireties, glassware, ceramic, plastic knobs, all that centrifugal architecture of a stove. Vegetable matter. No wonder painters go nuts. The way eye-tossed brain snaps to detail every time and the scene, all manner of message honking, not like a syntactical Dutch kitchen, yields no singularity long enough to say "There." "Stop putting smoke in my face!" "Wow. Did she hurt herself? What did she hurt?" I'm such a '40s/'50s person really, I always call it an icebox.

   The cat's eating Obi Wan and Babar's futzing with a padlock. The world, after all, needs a place to work. Did Dante misremember? Seeing the sky, demanding hills. Can this be America's lesson in love? "Be prosperous and nullify." Albeit minor intentions are seldom lost. (*Letter to Maria Gisborne.*) When from the Wish Star the Blue Fairy enters domestic space, the room goes blue, the star comes out on the end of her wand, the air sparkles. It's a small desert. You see a faint figure on the horizon — vaguely dishevelled, bottle in mouth, waving a shirt — probably your friend.

      That part of the room love's in looks good from here. A welcome tree at the yield sign, that's vital.

Broom Genealogy

Eventually I learn to distinguish between two kinds of broom plants, French and Scotch. Every time I take a walk with you I get to ask one question about plant life, although you say I always forget the answer next time around so my questions are repetitive like an absurdist play or catechism. Both French and Scotch broom are somehow naturally fixed in the mesa ground, the clay and sand and some real dirt of it, though the Scotch kind you generally find closer to the cliffs. Plain yellow flowers of the French come in fours, are aromatic and outnumbered by lighter green fuzzy leaves and wide flat pods. In the dry summers they crackle in the wind. I first heard that crackling sound beside the house you were living in when we first met, the Red House, so-called, on piers, with its porch and sliding glass doors, next to Martinelli's cow pasture. Scotch broom is tighter, wirier, darker, all stem, stalk and flower with no leaf, really broom-like. The Scotch broom flowers are a flashier yellow, often with a splash of red at the depths and lip. I thought they were like snapdragons but you said sweetpeas. The French invade every treeless plot, covering along with scrub oak and coyote bush the undeveloped ("unimproved") lots of the mesa. We have a wire fence at the rear edge of the backyard planted against their advance, which can be quick and insidious as Birnam Wood. Fibrous and dense and hard to clear, a machete is best to hack it with. You always say you forget the Jewish half of my background. But there I am with French-Scotch-Irish-Dutch-Russian-Jewish in a backgound nature, with some Choctaw (Olive) intermarriage on the side. One great-grandfather of Irish descent seems to have married first one sister then the other. As for the Jewish part, "the family (after Odessa). . . lived around Chicago always. William worked as a tailor for a large firm called Kuppenheimer for thirty years and was much beloved and a respected man . . ." The pin is diamond-shaped and edged with pearls. In the center, which is slightly raised, are the letters Z B T in gold on a black background, running along the short diagonal. Above the letters a skull and crossbones in white, and below is the six-pointed Star of David in light blue. The colors of the fraternity are light blue, white, and gold. Naturally, any background is fleeting, and love today, a forward love, is the only possible fixative that wears well. . . "We had brains enough, or were helpless enough, to stay with the reality of being for each other."

If I Pray to Anyone It Is to You

If I pray to anyone it is to you.
You make a U-turn & are immediately apprehended
By the power vested in me and taken away from you
Because you are minus identity at this moment
Where you linger
In a bad frame of mind
Like some weather on earth
Perpetually stained, and it looks like home.

So borrow a shiny pen
From the highway patrol
And see the boats, instant pairs
That idle steadily
On fortuitous tides.
A gray caulk-expanse for hammers,
As a lady takes a doughnut from a car trunk.
You never know what lands to the eye,
Seeing air stir water visibly.
But water comes to hide it.
Just a mole's margin of sand in any case.
And the nib flows.

On the High Window

Something to look at next to paint
sowbugs in vodka, purple buns
cyclist's boiling haze lifts
a target to its tilted edge
so spliffs the seens

I see a strange bare tree in the hollow
among the many mossy twists
its branches form a beast
that gnashes at the fog

seen is a point to which
at wonder
stance happens

wishing you a favorable career in Windex
mischeering the hoods

Space Dream

Broken headline column:

> YOU ARE GO
> ING TO END

Allen Ginsberg dives through the space hatch.
I watch him from the rim, hear his voice
trail a message "MAN ISSSSSSSSSSSSS. . . . . . ."
as he disappears through dot-hood.
The Poets — Anne Waldman, me, "all the poets" — float
in interstellar space, a substance I
can touch, a fine sheen. & then I'm up against the sun,
its soft orange neon glow. "THE SUN," I say, "IS BIG!"
Pause, & a chair sails silent past me into solar radiance.
"CHAIR INTO SUN!" I remark.
                              Then we are back on Earth,
speed skating on the silvery
                              Power Cones.

Young Manhattan

Wild things live in the room
I grew up in, the hum-whee-hum
of low-flying aircraft, their mission in 1951
to blow Manhattan to cinders, off the map

the simple clunk of the elevator cab
at the landing at the end of the long, long hall
shadows creeping every which way along the wall
seem and do, seem and do

15¹/₂/34

Good day, easing off, clouds moved
into every bright distance.
I like ease, how come?
With brushwork stays memory, your nose for a fact
long lured its winter clogs about.
Today cat yawns where yesterday it sneezed.
Right now it yawned. Into deluge reflection
roadside an orange cylinder divulges contents.
"Trashcan, see more at trash."
Solid matters dawn in questions of moment,
curios ample and lax
for ants to convene and pour over.
I didn't buy the book to rhyme or trounce
and now have staved off news, tides, self-delicacy.

Provincetown Light

Not the day Hans told Larry,
"You have got no talent for growing old!"
a plum branch of ribbons was lowered by Elaine
with Johnnie Walker Red to pastel Paul who beamed.

There was light in Provincetown then —
a shine on the method, mostly how pink
or wide the investment, should we ever have to deal
between Picasso and Matisse.

Missing

Who will verify the angles for this street-address
or take a capsule of the final tone of truck?

Scared when they don't answer, out past
the hour, and you prepared to play.

Is what we have here a way of stress or trade agreements
materialized off a major phylum's own late sets?

At dinner once my father called me "a pigeon for the Reds,"
and although as always our crystals clinked in kind,

I don't think in Mandarin.
I just wanted to kill my pillow or whatever it was.

Symmetrical fleshapods dot the pale glass roof.
The big guns robbed milady of her bath.

Amazing, there was no music before or during,
only abscesses of snow.

Wim Wenders takes it to the snow.
The guy with a drink bought it.

The patch denotes sex, but try and mouth
"fuck" sexily when nervous you keep spilling things.

Follow that crab through your usual alternate route.
No clerk can read a finger for the proper candidate.

A Pittsfield joker runs the human family off the road with
     his truck.
Maybelline wants to see something pretty before you catch the owl.

The duck may well return if your friend does.
I need someone to leap out in the dark upstairs.

The poet of particle board sees all veils collapse.
The workers' thought-process exposes the shark face of nations
     beneath an elevator shaft

Veteran dingalings applaud Earth's curfew from Nirvana Lodge.
Hook those tracers to a newt.

Liberty proposes the private army.
Soundproofings in the Capital, quite a day: "But we don't
     need you."

Meanwhile copper shellfish shatter into rounds
negotiable for time.

Take dire note of my back and woebegone brains in the river.
The swamp's remembrance is a human ramp.

The neighbors' chickens eat our snails.
Time is person, but what but destiny sweeps a room?

An orchid bears the twitch. My need is such.
You can still put a wheel around the far wall.

Missing (2)

Hopeless and helpless are the significant

                art forms of our age

and the interview

         likewise has its sting.

What is that mothball

          doing in the strawberries?

The boot splashes down

          hell-first to the shin.

The rest goes bouncing with Betty

              along the path to the bank.

I shit not knowing

        what else to be asked

        what might the sudden orders be

        when we bolt for the night.

How prompt.

          The wife allows as how she can't abide

that the goaded message

          falls from the knob,

but the kids say the flying

          remnants look neat,

favored as they are

        by just any transformation.

The law was this putz

        distributed through 50 states.

A few passes with the broom

        and the alphabet is gone.

I can stick with conceit

        or a standard stress

disfigured,

        but give me anytime the keen

vertebrate mindedness

        of Janice Rule.

A Fixture

Not ever knowing what she does in the shower,
a frictional sorrow like bedding in dark
feeling brows flex over wireless concerns,
not hers.
A stone in the river you can't move moves you.
And the postholes wobble. Glaze is permanent.

In her partition is the stairway of unhunched love,
a muscular mouth.

The Position

I have to work harder to maintain being all three persons.
I fool around with myself in the fields quite a bit, and come to
rest, rooted to the spot, for a long spell. Tending to go to all
places, the easy self-flagellatings of prolonged adolescence are
not what I'm after. I thought there must be some way I could
do something about it. So I got put aside. Simply minded, it
has not always been so: You can listen, talk, and so on, but
books seem to be signs of their despair. Pale logic notwithstanding, I will be enticed, I am not so rigorous that I cannot
be, where you are concerned, though never exactly falling for it.
I see you standing in the clear light. I've managed to travel
quite far by steady employment on the principles handed me.
Absolutely only my compliance has order, a fright wig I wear
on the inner sleeve of self-containment. I am not possessed. I
don't really have to work for a living. I forget names but their
circumstances never. My ears burn to intuit long-distance,
sitting in the face of, or dancing excerpted from, as it were, the
whole enchilada. I hate commas in the wrong places. They are
like dead flowers in poems in life. One hundred years from
this day, pow, right in the kisser! The man about town, the
family man and the clairvoyant are one. As performance goes,
it's fun like TV fun. I can drive this road blindfold.

Chaloff

In an instant the world seems fairly made of wood.
Balsa wood, and air. And song consists in passing
nothings around on a deck. The Pacific Ocean rests
upon a peak, and Boston is a bay. Honey dumps the flood,
burying the furlong granite ear. A multi-lunged, galumphing
chain of event stirs and stows the static —
mops, churns, hooks, and levels out.
Downstairs smells of polish remover.
In early autumn a butterfly kisses the goof.
He is able: "I once knew how to do this."

Motion was the first miracle,
followed by a bird act.
While it shines on the pointed hush's shameless order of mention,
a piano's gravity will see to acquiring a proper knife.
In tingles I catch the blandished coffee's murmur on a string,
hearing sowbugs scamper over flannel sheets.
You must soothe beasts first to be funk.

What's new? Maybe Chaloff wasn't. Anyhow, in Egyptian
Gardens his chorus recalls their dancing like a nut.
Night the one color of a vocalist's shirt
embosses coasters from its incline of a sort,
although Lower Slobovia is no way a state of music.
But such aloof floes make mockery of the continuous present.
Against the nub, the nebulous, his glazed twig
wiffles, woos, and wails,
striding an imported pressure the dew blapped.
Which twig holds night?
Who's only catastrophic?

The world and its cracks?
Wish, occlusion, force,
a practice out of fondest samplings, which fitfully bent beads.

Ode

1.
Midnight moonlight mobbed Dante's bridge
Nights you are arduous
to ward off cheap distress
anxiety earned like yesterday's pay
Correction can't dramatize itself
probably shouldn't
January passing maples in a car
provisionally bright alive
and at the controls
wrong, no worries, except
motion prevaricates
there isn't much of it
in the right places
a little of who you are
suspected to involve
If I could I would do so out of excess
not necessarily a bad thing
cue me and I'm on
clue me in and I'm yours
now I'm going to name that tune
suggest a title, indicate
strongest love-and-hate scenario
first sign of spring
first serious encounter
by chance with the rich and strange
Whoever scribbled white markings
on the floor at our feet
was shameless and
lacked character

I'm just peeing in the wind
meaning resilient, dizzy and frayed
rain hammers pearls
on the skylights
in a pair of red rainboots
decalcomania
under ordinarily visible
penises and breasts
One house actually had a barometer
although it never did any work
neither rising nor falling
the steady-as-she-goes
on the surface of the wall in the grand
living room behind the sofa
in a well-polished mahogany frame
Easy does or easy doesn't
Inspirited takes care of fathoms dense
with passing hims and hers
massed around the alcove
"Watch the hook. Beware the hook."
Hemming a summit
pulsing white tusk, sky's maritime dray
"Bub!" my father's voice, wristbone shivers
dreamed I hopped off a big white truck
Queens Boulevard and lost my gear

2.
sunlight fractures the plexiglas
fanning around sturdy trunks and boughs
sly shadows of bush in the yard high noon
cow trails wild thought has mapped
rain sorrow brainsweat and fatigue
eagerness of insane

whomsoever eyes take in and fix
requiring required
coordinated gales of laughter light and love
on the way home from the sleepyheaded doctor's office
a fish that eats
birds that freak in unison
bugs at their labors
do the dirty work
a rapid boil
politesse du coeur
politeness of or from the heart
in the assembled body
assuming the bodily appearance
of a body of two
the small boy rolls some marbles around
on the floor of the house
one gets lost
a pointless story
but suffused
with recognizable colors
that travel far
time is important
making as it does
elbow-room for happenings of note
to occupy quasi-permanent niches
in estimable space
probably you knew all this
because something tells us
as is its wont
and the occasional savage trance-like state
of people in the process of singing
being heard

Chocolate Chocolate Chip

Forgoing intellect in favor of a brighter style
Would be more better efficacious if the bed were higher
The wind is back battering the trees for more
Light, eyeballing sanity in brilliance of depth

One luckless beetle met its porch death
In daylight that had been airborne
We admired its enamelled frame, had beers and fucked
Deep in a friend's house cloyed with devices

If I own a hat these are the bands well-appointed
In the sorry story of finding the world
Managed in footfalls of sworn neglect
Spelling each other through the glaze and sheens and rapid tide.

Under a Cloud and After the Waves

real winter flips
lugging the year bed

reverses no mean can evade
Dagwood corrugates

he stood raving from the dance
solution primed under no bottle

went for the shoe
it was barely awake

latched onto a big fast bus
his flailing tongues to ride the lunar

each far-flung crate before you useless
but that furrowed head

pounces drawn
and as betoned

after Lyn Hejinian

Night Straits

Awake I'm freed
or stored in even attics
I relapse to bare need
fall blinking up from
the wall not like dark
an empty pocket away
from which loss I started

Nothing leaves my face
except the mean feet
of sponges, bases varnished
with smoke-filled rocks, the deadening
oddball zeroing in on the unmarked
every bit as deductible
as they are dumb

Bulbs lock the dark mutes to impervious lengths
the yoking of salt to soda
but this part of a parlor couldn't stroke their idles
lulling the rider to his pint

Waking pursued by a vapor
loaded out of a foreground still
unnerved plenty against a curve
in the night, and I'm its trust
I sit for hours

after Clark Coolidge

At the Skin
for Francesco Clemente

This living underfoot
pale woven weaponry
to each its
planetary influences
ever on the mark
exceptionalizing
capable, probably culpable
I am turning 50, a worker ant
getting a grip on
the spirit graph of Florida, Maine,
Queenie the dachshund
and the several areas to the left of
sketchily Urdu
the reasonable pretense.

The tattered movie screen has taught us to question our betters
the truth of it is it isn't butter
and you can't get a grave on a bun

but the pinwheel releases a lot of costly packaging
that helps the light
in elegiac lengths
become extrinsic
like almost pure.

Chasing the Slip

What choice have I to lift as mallet to my stake?
There's a hair in your pine, muddle,
Impeding the switches of I never do decide.
Nuts to this bulge of condition then, that doubt word,
With stiller things backlit against its peaks. . .

When a woman looks at a plant I walk behind
In boldface, noodling every twig that leans,
The wear and tear and slash and burn
Her fabric audits; and when a name escapes,
Animate in fog, I dub it.

Serenade

Moon comes up, tide goes out.
Your logic is held together

Like by a headband.
Fronting the Painted Desert,

A recalcitrant ocean pounds.
Houses block or frame the view.

In a hurry always, utterly remote,
You insist or stumble into interest.

Either way, another chance to look,
Not to mention what ordinarily happens.